A+ GUIDE TO GREAT GRADES

by

Louise Colligan

TELEMACHUS
PRESS

A+ GUIDE TO GREAT GRADES

Cover designed by Kit Menis

Cover Art Kit Menis
Images by Kit Menis

ISBN# 978-1-937387-88-4 (eBook)
ISBN# 978-1-937387-89-1 (Paperback)

Published by: Telemachus Press, LLC
Visit our website: http://www.telemachuspress.com

Version 2011.12.05

Printed in the United States of America
10 9 8 7 6 5 4 3 2 1

Table of Contents

1

Getting It Together in the Middle Grades

Remember the good old days when you were in the lower grades? You probably had one main teacher for most of the day. You knew your way around. Every third Wednesday was baked chicken day. Every first Friday of the month school let out early for teacher meetings. Everybody knew everybody else. Each day in the lower grades was pretty much like the day before—predictable.

That was then. School is probably a lot more unpredictable now that you've hit the middle grades. Instead of one main teacher, you may have three or four of them. That doesn't count the gym teacher who looks and talks like an NFL football coach. Some of

the older students do, too. A few of them are
giants who tower over the kids in your new
grade. That means you!

And why didn't your older sister warn
you that every single kid in middle school is
a different size, even kids you knew last year?
Do they even serve baked chicken at the cafeteria? And by the way, where is the cafeteria?
Maybe your middle school is so overcrowded,
it follows a rotating schedule on Tuesdays
and Thursdays when your lunch periods fall
at two o'clock. What's up with that? Not to
mention that a couple classes take place in a
trailer miles from your locker. On some days,
you barely have time to grab your books, race
through slush, mud, or rain to get to class on
time.

Middle-grade situations like these can
really stress you out. You do your homework
but forget it on the bus. That bus is late one
morning, so you miss the announcement about
a social studies quiz the next day. You listen in
class but run out of paper to take notes. So you
write an important deadline on the palm of
your hand then wash your hands by mistake!
Pretty soon these mini disasters snowball.
You just miss the mark, not out of laziness or

dead brain cells. You just aren't sure how to get it together—the schedules, the notebooks, the announcements, deadlines, handouts, and supplies. Help is on the way!

Real Students, Real Advice

Look at what these middle grade survivors had to say when asked: "What was the hardest thing you remember about starting middle school?"

> " . . . *knowing where the classes were.*"
> " . . . *getting used to older kids.*"
> " . . . *being teased by eighth graders.*"
> " . . . *switching from class to class.*"
> " . . . *having too many teachers.*"
> " . . . *getting my locker opened.*"
> " . . . *having too many subjects.*"
> " . . . *learning my schedule.*"
> " . . . *figuring out what class came next.*"
> " . . . *doing homework in all different subjects.*"
> " . . . *keeping my locker neat.*"

Well, guess what? Small steps can make the middle grades easier. Here's what these same middle grade survivors answered when asked: "Now that you've been in middle school for a while, what advice would you give to new students just starting the middle grades?"

> *"Don't fall asleep in class!"*
> *"Pay attention."*
> *"Reread everything."*
> *"Save all your notes and the teachers' handouts."*
> *"Don't be nervous. It'll get better."*
> *"Be on time."*
> *"Don't do your homework or study for a test at the last minute."*
> *"Don't be obnoxious."*
> *"Don't worry about it. Just do it."*
> *"Take notes."*
> *"Don't aggravate older kids."*
> *"Don't worry if you don't make friends the first day."*
> *"You'll get used to it."*
> *"Do your work all the time. Don't let it pile up."*
> *"Don't worry about other kids. Just be yourself. If they're really going to be your friends, they'll accept you that way."*

*"Don't be afraid to ask your teacher
   things."*
"Don't show off."
"Stay home!"
"Be organized."
"It gets easier."

The checklist below is a plan for revving up some of those good habits right now. First identify the A+ good things you do at home already. Then decide which A+ good moves you want to work on. Here goes:

The Are-You-Ready-for-the Middle-Grades Quiz

Check "Yes" or "No" next to each item below.

YES NO

❑   ❑   I lay out school clothes and my backpack in the same place on school nights.

❑   ❑   I get at least ten hours of sleep a night, especially on school nights.

❑   ❑   I have an alarm clock to wake myself up in the morning.

❑ ❑ I try to eat something healthy for breakfast, lunch, snacks, and dinner.

❑ ❑ I use a timer to manage work and fun.

❑ ❑ I'm usually on time for the bus or for school.

❑ ❑ I have a backpack or tote bag to haul my books and school supplies.

❑ ❑ I clean out my backpack every week so I can find my stuff.

❑ ❑ I use an assignment pad or planner to write down all my homework.

❑ ❑ I have a binder divided by subjects or separate subject notebooks for each class.

❑ ❑ I usually pack the right class notebooks and books I will need for school or home.

❑ ❑ I have a special study area at home with supplies, a dictionary, bulletin board, calendar, and folders to save old tests, corrected homework, and teacher handouts.

❑ ❑ I have copies of my school schedule at home, at school, and in my back pack.

❑ ❑ I have a back-and-forth folder for papers my parent needs to see or sign.

❑ ❑ I have the phone number or e-mail of someone in each of my classes in case I'm out sick.

❑ ❑ I control the amount of time I spend on video games, computers, TV, and phones so they don't suck too much time away from school work.

Which "No" habits would you like to turn into "Yes" habits? That's your personalized A+ plan! Start with small, easy steps. Master each A+ good move before you go on to the next one. If one step is too hard, try a different one. Don't try to change yourself overnight, or nobody will recognize you!

Believe it or not, your muscles, as well as your brain, will help you form memories and habits. For example, when you carry your backpack to your study space instead of throwing it down any old place when you get home, something new happens. After a few days, as soon as you walk in the door, your brain will kick in with a reminder: "Backpack in room." Really! Habits become automatic the more you repeat them. Once that autopilot thing clicks on, "It gets easier," just as one of those wise middle school kids said.

2

A+ You Shape Up

You can line up your books in your locker by color, file all your old tests, sharpen all your pencils but still struggle at school if you feel tired, headachy, and stressed out. Sleep, healthy foods, and regular exercise aren't just for sports jocks but for brain jocks, too. So before you start color-coding your notebooks, first take care of your beautiful, handsome A+ self.

Get Your Zzzs On

Don't faint, but do you know that if you're between the ages of nine and twelve, you should be getting at least 10 hours or more of sleep a night? That's how much sleep time your brain needs to release certain chemicals, called hormones. When you're zonked out during the night, a part of your brain is busy. It's sending signals to different organs in your body to produce hormones and other chemicals your body needs to be in tip-top shape.

These important substances do many jobs. They repair worn-out cells. They make you grow. They control your moods and appetite. And they store information and experiences from your day into your memory. These sleep-time activities are important to your health—and to your school life. This kind of healthy sleep isn't something you can cram into weekends. Your body needs to go through its many sleep cycles every single night so that your brain can get all those good hormones flowing.

Not only does the right amount of sleep make you bigger, stronger, smarter, and less cranky, something else happens. Your body's immune system, which fights off infections, recharges during sleep. Many sleep studies show that students who don't get enough sleep get sicker and miss more school than people who get the right amount of sleep for their age.

Ten hours or more of sleep time may seem impossible. How are you ever going to get that much if you have to go to school, clean the birdcage, do homework, make your bed, talk to your friends, practice flute, soccer, ballet, and learn a part for the school play?

Take charge of your bedtime! Here's how to become an A+ sleeper:

- **Figure out your perfect bedtime.** Subtract ten hours from the time you usually leave for school each morning. If you leave your house at 7:30 AM, and you need a half hour to get ready for school, your bedtime should be ten hours earlier, 9:00 PM. If you leave for school later, you can stay up later.

- **Plan your work and playtimes.** If your bedtime is 9:00 PM, add up the time it takes to complete your after-school activities, homework, and chores. That might be two hours for soccer, fifteen minutes to walk the dog, a half hour to eat dinner, an hour of homework, and so forth. Subtract all these "must-do" blocks of time from the number of after-school hours you have. The leftover times are free "you times." Sometimes you'll have more free time and sometimes less. If a great TV program is on one night, that might mean less instant messaging with your best friend, just for that night. If you have a ton of homework on a certain night, tell everyone you're "going underground" until the next day. If you have too many activities, talk to your family about cutting back on some of them.

Lots of kids in the middle grades have trouble getting to sleep. They wind up like zombies the next day. Here's how to banish the zombie from the bedroom:

- **Avoid long naps.** Long naps—more than a half hour—during the day rob you of nighttime sleep.

- **Avoid snacking after dinner.** Your body shouldn't be doing two jobs at bedtime. It needs to be fixing cells and producing hormones, not digesting corn chips. Avoid exercise too close to bedtime for the same reason. Your body needs to be in sleep mode, not muscle mode, at nighttime.

- **Dim the lights and turn off the tech toys such as the television, phones, video games, and computers a half hour before bedtime.** Your body is sensitive to light and darkness. Less light triggers certain brain chemicals, which bring on that cozy feeling of nighttime sleepiness.

- **Ask a parent or older sibling to pull up the shades after you fall asleep or early in the morning.** The morning light will activate your wake-up chemicals. Some heavy sleepers use special alarm clocks that wake them up with sound *and* light.

- **Roll back your bedtime by half an hour if you suffer from daytime tiredness.** Keep rolling it back until you wake up feeling rested. Many students your age need more than 10 hours of sleep.

- **Follow the same going-to-bed habits every night.** That way your body learns how to wind down automatically. Follow the same sleep schedule as much as possible on weekends. Sleeping too late on Saturdays and Sundays can really throw off your sleep cycles.

- **When you're ready for bed, sink back on your pillow and drift away!**

Feed Your Brain

Humans love salty, sweet, fatty foods. So have some in small amounts. But first make sure you fill up with the kinds of high-test, healthy foods that make you strong and smart the way healthy sleep does.

Certain kinds of foods help you feel full longer than fatty, salty, sugary junk foods do. Start your school day with filling healthy foods that won't quit on you in math class halfway through the morning. Fix or choose healthy foods for breakfast and lunch. These include whole grains like real oatmeal and cereals, whole wheat breads, muffins, and crackers.

All the cells in our bodies, especially brain cells, need something called protein, which you can get from small amounts of meat, eggs, fish, milk, yogurt, low-fat cheeses, beans, nuts, or foods made out of soy. Power foods also include fresh and dried fruits, along with green, red, yellow, and orange veggies. Healthy foods at regular meal and snack times prevent those sudden junk-food munchie attacks.

Healthy snacks and meals aren't all you need. Your body is made up of water, so drink up—four to six glasses a day. If you're eating right, you don't need fancy vitamin drinks or energy drinks to stay healthy. Good old plain water works just fine. Headache experts say that people who have regular sleep habits, eat healthy meals and snacks at the same time every day, and drink plenty of water can prevent many headaches.

Move Your Bones

The great thing about exercise is that it revs you up *and* relaxes you. After-school exercise is great way to get yourself out of sitting-in-class mode into muscle mode. You don't have to be a super jock to exercise. Just find some activity that gets you moving. Walk home from school if you have a friend to walk with, it's safe, and you have a parent's permission. Run around with your dog in the backyard. Learn new dance moves. Have fun playing outdoor games with your friends and sibs. Try to balance couch-potato activities, such as watching TV or playing video games, with equal amounts of physical activities.

Stress Busters

You know what stress is, right? It's that panicky, worried feeling that something bad is about to happen. Your heart races, and you feel jumpy. Those physical feelings are real. So are stress-caused headaches, stomachaches, and muscle aches. When you feel anxious, your brain releases stress hormones. These rev up the body to move it out of danger. Stress hormones were helpful in prehistoric times when humans faced wild animals and other dangers. And they're helpful if someone needs to jump away from an out-of-control car. Unfortunately, students' worries about school, problem friends or family members, tests, and more, can sometimes bring on that heart-pounding, revved-up feeling at the wrong time.

So how can you deal with worries? Stressed out people often feel they have no control over anything—that bad things can happen out of the blue. That's why taking charge of small things in your daily life can give you power. Work out a bedtime that always leaves you rested and in a decent mood. Figure out how long things actually take. Then add a little more time so you don't feel rushed or anxious. Schedule your time so that you get a good balance of work, play, and rest. Organize your possessions so that you can always find them. Work on projects in small chunks. Give yourself plenty of breaks while you work and afterward, too. Share your worries with people you trust. Family members, a favorite teacher, school counselor, or close friends can help relieve you of some worries.

Okay, so what happens once you turn into a rested, oatmeal-veggie-fruit-eating-water-drinking-exercising, deep-breathing A+ physical specimen? You're ready to take on school from the home front.

3

Organizing Home Life

Did an evil wind blow through your room and deposit your class books in one corner, your school supplies under the bed, and your clarinet under a pile of socks? It's time to find a good home for these orphans.

Every student needs a junk-free, pile-free zone for school stuff no matter what the rest of the room looks like. This at-home school center can be a corner, a wall, a desk and chair, or a couple of shelves just for school things. It's where you'll always find school supplies, your next day's school clothes, your backpack, schoolbooks, musical instruments, or sports equipment. Your school space doesn't need to be in your room if there's a good, quiet space somewhere else in your house or apartment.

At-Home School Zone

To set up your at-home school zone, get a trash bag, recycling bag or box, a half-dozen folders (or, better, an accordion folder with lots of slots), and two or three plastic bins or shoeboxes. Here's how to set up your own at-home school zone.

- **Toss.** Throw all outdated school papers, invitations, and magazines into the recycling bin. Pitch into the trash bag dried-out pens, crayons, and markers, along with worn-down pencils, and other trash.

- **Sort.** Group all your school papers—handout sheets, notes, and corrected homework and tests—by subject to file later in subject folders. Sort all your schoolbooks and notebooks by subject, too.

- **Move it.** Everything that isn't school-related belongs in other parts of your room or home. Move all your clothes out of your school zone into the closet, dresser drawers, or laundry bin. From now on, the only items that get to live in your school zone are your next day's clothes, backpack, and school-related materials.

- **Shelve.** Create shelf space for storing all your schoolbooks when you're home.
- **File.** Set aside all your sorted paperwork to put into folders.

Once you've cleared out your school zone space of nonschool things, here's what to add to it:

- **A half-dozen folders or an accordion folder with slots for each subject.** Use the folders to store, by date, corrected homework, old quizzes, and teacher handouts for each of your subjects. Folders are your go-to source of study materials for tests.

- **Set aside one "Back and Forth" folder to keep in your backpack.** Put permission slips, invitations, and other important non-subject papers you and your parents need to see or sign in your "Back and Forth" folder.

- **Bulletin board, magnetic board, or whiteboard**. Put your calendar on or near whatever kind of display board you have. Stick on tickets, invitations, and any other important paperwork related to school, social, and family events.

- **Wall calendar**. This is the place to keep track of your busy life from now on. Circle the super-important dates in big red letters. Write down every deadline or appointment as it comes up—from after-school dates to test deadlines— from orthodontist appointments to band practice. If you're a techie, schedule appointments and school deadlines on a computer calendar. Schedule the program to send you e-mails to alert you to important deadlines.

- **Extra class schedule**. Put this on your bulletin board, too, so that you can check what classes you have the next day. Don't you want to know you have a free period after lunch so you can get some homework done then instead of right now?

- **The phone number of one student in each class.** When you miss a class or get stuck on homework, call for help.

- **A flat surface to write on.** This can be a desk, a piece of shelving resting on cinder blocks, or a clipboard to put over your knees (if you do your best writing in bed or sitting on the floor).

- **School supplies.** Keep a stash of tape, scissors, markers, glue, pens, pencils, craft materials for projects, thumb-tacks or pushpins, clips, extra notebook paper, sticky notes, and index cards to make your own flash cards for tests. Store all this in a spare drawer, bin, or box so you can find supplies fast without searching all over the house. Other great things to have: a dictionary, the-saurus, and library card; a wristwatch; a tape recorder to help you memorize spelling and vocabulary lists, multipli-cation tables, and math rules.

- **Three-ring binder with pocket dividers for each subject or different-colored subject notebooks**. Use your binder or notebooks to take class notes and to store teacher handouts to bring home. Write your name and phone number in each of your notebooks.

- **Small assignment pad or planner**. Use this to write down each of your daily homework assignments and due dates. Many students clip this to the inside covers of their three-ring notebooks. Write your name and phone number in your assignment pad or planner.

- **A pencil case with a few pens, markers, erasers, pencil sharpener, highlighter**. Give yourself bonus points if you have a clear pencil case so you can see if you need to restock. Add extra bonus points if you get the kind with three holes that can fit into a binder.

- **An empty backpack**. From now on, all schoolbooks and notebooks belong in one of three places—your backpack, your at-home school zone, or in your locker at school. Notice that sentence did

not include the words, "under the bed."
Put your schoolbooks and notebooks in
the main section of your backpack. Zip
it shut (unless you have to store your
lunch with your books). Everything else
goes in separate pockets—the same
pockets every time. If you have a pencil
case that isn't attached to your binder,
find a home for it in its own pocket. Use
another pocket for personal items you
like to have at school, such your wallet,
bus pass, tissues, Band-aids, and hand
wipes. Don't leave home without them!

- **Alarm clock**. The loudest alarm clock
  sounds better than a loud human.

- **Timer**. Control your time so it doesn't
  get away from you. Use your timer to
  follow the A+ 20/10 Homework Method.
  More about that later in Chapter 6.

If you do many of these A+ good home moves,
you can practically go on cruise control.

Ten Totally Worth It Time Savers

Everyone has the same 24 hours of day and night. But if you wish you could get more done in that time, try these tips:

- **Do family chores at the same time every day.**

- **Set up your next day's breakfast and lunch the night before.**

- **Shower or wash your hair after school sports or at night instead of in the morning.**

- **If a task only takes a few minutes, do it on the spot.** Examples: get a permission slip signed, or file that day's teacher handouts.

- **Update your wall calendar every day.**

- **Schedule bathroom times.** To avoid fights over who's using the bathroom, use it at specific times. Do hair-combing and dressing in your room.

- **Avoid family arguments in the morning.** It takes up too much time and ruins your day. You can always finish an argument later, but you can't catch the school bus later.

- **Do as much homework as you can in school during free periods, lunchtime, or on the bus.** But if school hours are the only time to see your friends, save your homework for home.

- **Line up school notebooks and textbooks in class order in your bookbag or in your locker so you can grab them fast.**

- **Use your timer to plan tech playtimes.** Instead of channel surfing, check your favorite program schedules ahead of time and just watch those. Use your timer to remind yourself when it's time to unplug from tech toys. Ask someone about putting blocking software on the computer to limit Internet surfing. Work out regular calling times with your friends so that you can have lots of fun talking or texting without that English or social studies assignment hanging over you.

Now that you've gotten your home life in shape, hop on the A+ bus. We're going to school!

4
Organizing School Life

It's 8:29 AM. You made it out of your house in record time. Your backpack contains your completed homework, books, pencils, the healthy lunch you made last night, and your flute. (You remembered your flute because you wrote down "band practice" on your wall calendar.) You are so organized for school, you can hardly believe it. You lean back in your seat. No way will Ms. Qwizwell, your science teacher, catch you off guard without your notebook again.

And for once, you have that vocabulary handout right where you can find it. Mr. Wordley, your language arts teacher, can go right ahead and ask you what *ornery* means. You even remembered to bring in the three dollars you need to go on the planetarium trip. According to this book, you should be all set for the day.

So why do you wish today were Saturday? Probably because you're wondering just how having a neat notebook with colored dividers is going to get you better grades. Or how your teacher's supposed to know you've made three copies of your schedule. You may be wondering how being organized at home is going to have any effect on this bell-ringing, crowded, noisy, and demanding place. School.

Well, having a copy of your schedule everywhere you go, always having your notebook, saving and filing all your handouts, writing down absolutely everything—these habits *do* pay off. They mean you're not playing catch-up or running around looking for things and being late for classes.

Now it's time to add a few good in-school habits to make your school day run like the school clocks. Identify which A+ at-school good moves you already do. Then decide which moves you want to work on.

Quiz Yourself on Organizing at School

Check off "Yes" or "No" next to each item below.

YES NO

❑   ❑ I usually arrive at school with everything I need that day.

❑   ❑ I figured out my locker combination by practicing over and over.

❑   ❑ My locker is so organized, I can grab everything I need in seconds.

❑   ❑ I keep a few school supplies in my locker in case I run out.

❑   ❑ I have my class schedule taped inside my locker so I have the books I need for the next class.

❑   ❑ I clean out my locker regularly.

❑   ❑ I am usually on time for my classes.

Do you already do all these A+ moves? Applause, applause. Go straight to Chapter 5. If you haven't quite become the master of your locker or the school clock, read on.

Locker Makeover

Lockers are your home away from home. You don't want to be locked out of your house, do you? You're not alone if you find yourself frantically whirling your combination in between classes, and the thing still doesn't open. And since your locker is your home away from home, keep it organized. That way you can always find what you're looking for in a hurry. Here are A+ solutions for organizing your locker:

- **Practice your combination**. During your free time, try to get your locker open several times in a row. Keep practicing until you hear that satisfying little click that says: "Open Sesame." In a secret place, keep a copy of the combination numbers.

- **Carry around what you need for the morning or afternoon**. That way you avoid locker madness in between classes. Definitely carry all the materials you need for faraway classes.

- **Buy a stackable locker shelf**. Line up textbooks and notebooks in class order on the shelf so you can see and grab them ASAP. Store everything else in small boxes or small plastic bins below the main shelf.

- **Tape your class schedule inside your locker door.** Double-check it when you're rushed for the next class and can't even *think*.

- **Store backup supplies, notebook paper, and toiletries in small plastic bins or boxes**. Extra school supplies prevent teacher dagger stares if you happened to run out of paper or your pen goes dry. Band-aids and tissues prevent germs from spreading through the school—along with hand washing, that is.

- **Clean out the pantry cabinet and fridge in your locker**. Yes, keep today's lunch in your locker, but not last month's! Banish anything that was once alive, such as apple cores or orange peels. Begone broken cookies, crumbly muffins, and gummy power bars! Bring home handouts and corrected tests and homework for filing. They'll come in handy as study guides for future tests. Throw out all trash once a week.

Watch the Clock

Students often forget how short a 3-minute break is. Three minutes, or five, is probably enough time to get to class directly. But it's way too short to catch up on the latest gossip with your friends. Nothing is more aggravating to teachers than making an announcement and having two or three kids drift in late (or rush in, out of breath, and knocking things over as they race to their seats). Being late for class, arriving empty-handed, sitting there like a lump of clay, or chatting up a storm bring out the grouch in most teachers.

School Tools

Going to school is a job. Carpenters have saws and hammers; mechanics have wrenches; and teachers have briefcases and red markers. Students need special equipment, too: the class textbook, your binder or subject notebooks, an assignment pad or planner, writing materials, and the current completed homework assignment. These are your tools. If you show up empty-handed, you might as well tattoo a sign on your forehead that says: "I don't care!" You wouldn't be reading these words right now if you didn't care. So get it together—the class book, notebook, assignment pad, pens and pencils. Stash it all in your backpack, with extras in your locker. Show up for your job properly equipped.

5

How to Survive Any Class

Have you ever wondered why you can't just send in a tape recorder or video cam to record your classes while you stay home and catch up on sleep or a few DVDs? Actually, in most places you can take online classes if, for some reason, you can't physically go to school. So why do most students attend real live classes?

Back-and-forth questions connect teachers and students. Interacting students often come up with great group solutions and projects. On-the-spot feedback gives teachers a chance to repeat material or move ahead. Participating in real, live class discussions helps you remember material.

Listen Up

Does your mind go blank five minutes after class starts? Do your classes seem to be all talk with no point? When you study for tests, is it hard to remember what your teacher said was important? You don't need a hearing test, just a few tips on how to listen:

- **Be on time**. Most teachers start each class by announcing what they are going to cover in class: "Today we're going to talk about . . . " That's the big idea for that day. If you stroll in late, you'll miss it.

- **Arrive with all your homework done and questions about material you don't understand.** Homework prepares you for what the teacher is going to talk about.

- **Open your notebook and assignment book as soon as you sit down**. Write down any questions that come up as the teacher is talking. Then ask your questions before class is over.

- **Make eye contact with your teacher**. You'll find it easier to concentrate and follow along if you look right at your teacher. Watching the teacher keeps you from daydreaming or noticing that your best friend is clowning around. If you're allowed to choose your own seat, sit near the front. It's easier to hear what's going on. And you won't be as distracted by other kids sitting behind you.

- **Listen for clues**. "The main reason(s) is . . ." "The definition is . . ." "The main event to remember is . . ." "The most important fact is . . ." "To sum up . . ."

- **Listen for repetition, rephrasing, and summaries**. Teachers often repeat important material in different ways then sum it up.

- **Get in the game**. Ask questions. Answer questions. Take notes.

- **If you wear glasses, wear them**! Seeing clearly will help you listen better.

- **Find a study buddy for each class**. On a bad day, a daydream day, or a sick day, a study buddy can back you up with class notes. Return the favor.

If you do all these things, you'll be too busy to get caught staring at the clock, passing secret notes, or whispering with the kid next to you.

Take Note

In the middle grades, you usually don't have to write down too many class notes. But when you do, here's how to write good ones:

- **Write down the date on each set of notes and handout sheets**.

- **Draw a line or fold your notebook sheet 3 inches from the left edge**. Write main ideas or questions in a few words on the left side of the line or fold. Write related details on the right side.

- **Clump ideas together**. If your teacher talks about the importance of Paul Revere's ride in the American Revolution, write down "Paul Revere's Ride" on the left side of the line or fold on your notebook sheet. To the right, list the details the teacher mentions— the historical date, what happened and where, why the event happened, and the result. Then write the next new main idea on the left side of the line or fold and the related ideas on the right.

- **Write key words, not whole sentences.** List names, dates, phrases about what event happened, where it happened, and why. List numbered or lettered steps in just a few words.

- **Picture it**. If you're a visual person, create a mind map instead of regular notes. Write down "Paul Revere's Ride," and circle it. Then draw branches from the circle. Write down a few details about Paul Revere's ride on each branch. Start a new mind map for each main subject the teacher talks about.

- **Save all handout sheets**. Follow the information on each handout as your teacher talks about it. Use highlighters, markers, and stars to mark up whatever your teacher says is important on the handout. One secret about handouts is that they contain most of the questions—and answers—that will be on your homework and many of your tests.

The other secret is that any teacher who has stood in line for the school copier when he or she could be in the teacher's lounge thinks the handout information is pretty important. So save them all. File them at home by date and subject for test time.

- **Write it down**. If your teacher says, "Write it down," write it down. That means the information is important. Underline it, too.

- **Copy this**. If your teacher writes something on the board or says, "Copy this," copy it.

- **Highlight important information**. On your own notes, circle and underline any information your teacher says is going to be on a test. Don't forget the lightning bolts and stars!

- **Borrow another student's notes or handouts if you missed a class or were daydreaming**. See a study buddy or your teacher about any missing notes or assignments when you return to Planet Earth.

- **Write down the homework assign- ment, tests, and due date in your assignment pad or planner.**

Okay, now you know what to do about your school things. But what do you do about peo- ple at school—the ones who can make school life hard? How do you "organize" them?

Class Comedians and Other Distractions

Do you know these students? The pilot is the kid who takes the teacher's handouts and turns them into sleek aircraft. The whisperer carries on 40-minute conversations without getting distracted by the sound of a teacher's voice. The note passer sends forth yesterday's gos- sip on little slips of paper. The noisemaker has perfected all the sounds of the animal king- dom and turns the class into a zoo. The come- dian can't resist just one more joke. Do some of these characters sound a little too familiar? They make it hard for everyone else to pay attention in class. Kids who clown around are often the very students having trouble in school. That's why they act up. Try not to be that kid's sidekick in class. You can applaud the class clown's performance outside of class.

Hard teachers

Sooner or later, it happens. You get a teacher who is hard to get along with. What do you do?

- **Be extra-prepared for a hard teacher's class**. A teacher can't complain that you haven't done your homework if you have.

- **Turn in neat, complete homework.** A teacher can't tell you your work is sloppy if it's neat and complete.

- **Show up on time, prepared, and sit there quietly taking notes.** A teacher can't hassle you about your behavior if you do a perfect imitation of an A+ student.

- **Take a deep breath and count to ten.** If a teacher seems to pick on you and your usual reaction is to talk back, breathe deeply and listen until the rant is over.

- **Talk with a teacher you trust or with one of your parents.** They may have some advice about dealing with the hard teacher.

Hard Subjects

Suppose one reason you hate a certain class is because you don't understand the work. That's enough to make you crawl under the covers on a Monday morning, isn't it? Here are some tips to get through a hard class:

- **Spend twice as much study time on a hard class as on an easy one.**
- **Do the hardest homework first**. That's when you are most alert.
- **Ask the teacher to repeat explanations of hard material or assignments.**
- **See the teacher after class if you still need help.** When a teacher knows you're really trying, he or she may give you extra help.
- **Find a friend in class who is good in the subject.** See if he or she can explain it to you more simply.

- **Write down the homework assignments, word for word.**

- **Take class notes**. Find a study buddy in class and compare notes.

- **Ask a librarian if there's an available video or an easier book on the subject.**

- **Check homework help Web sites on the Internet.** Some of them might explain the subject more clearly than your teacher does. Many YouTube videos explain school subjects in simple ways. If some Web sites give you extra practice tests, try doing them for 5 or 10 minutes or so every day.

- **Master material before you move on to the next chapter, section, or idea.**

- **Have someone look over your homework.** An older brother or sister, a parent, or a student who is good in the subject can sometimes explain material in a way that works for you.

- **Reread all corrected homework, tests, and papers in a hard class.** You should do this for all your subjects. But reviewing is even more important in a tough class than an easier one. Save all your work so you can identify what keeps tripping you up.

- **If your teacher or parent suggests a tutor, sign up!** Also sign up for any after-school help your school offers. Yes, extra work can be a pain, but it will pay off. Fix the problem early while it's still manageable and hasn't turned into a monster yet. Hang in there! You can do it!

6

How to Do Homework

It gets on the bus with you. When you open the door, it follows you inside. It whispers in your ear when you try to get away from it. What is this shadow that follows you around 24/7? Homework. Here's what a group of middle grade students had to say about it:

> *"If only we didn't have homework."*
> *"Oh, no, I forgot my homework again!"*
> *"I did my homework, but it's a mess."*
> *"I can't watch TV 'til I do my homework."*
> *"I can't go out 'til I do my homework."*
> *"My life would be perfect if only I didn't have homework."*

Sound familiar? If there's one thing nearly every student complains about, it's homework. Ten out of ten middle school kids would probably rather get no homework than have hot fudge sundaes at lunch every day.

Since homework can be a big pain, let's see how to ease that pain. First, take a look at what works and doesn't work for you when it comes to homework. In the quiz below, are there some A+ good moves you do already? Hooray. Now focus on the steps you can do to take the sting out of homework pain.

Quiz Yourself on Homework

Check "Yes" or "No" next to each item below.

At school:

YES   NO

- ❑   ❑   I write down all my assignments and deadlines.
- ❑   ❑   I ask the teacher questions about parts of the homework I'm not sure about.
- ❑   ❑   Before I leave class, I reread my assignment pad so I know what books and papers I need to bring home.

At home:

❑ ❑ I have figured out the best time of day to schedule my homework.

❑ ❑ I write down future projects and test deadlines on my wall calendar.

❑ ❑ I check my wall calendar every day to see if any deadlines are coming up soon.

❑ ❑ I usually don't postpone doing homework.

❑ ❑ I work on the hardest homework first to get it out of the way.

❑ ❑ I use a timer to do my homework in small chunks, then give myself short breaks.

❑ ❑ I do my homework in quiet parts of the house without watching television or answering the phone until I take a break.

❑ ❑ I write down questions about parts of the homework I don't under stand.

❑   ❑ I have a friend or someone in my family I can ask about homework I don't understand.

❑   ❑ I reread each assignment when I finish it. I check that it is neat and complete, and has the right punc tuation and spelling.

❑   ❑ I check my assignment pad when I finish my homework to check if I have done all of it.

❑   ❑ I put my homework and books in my backpack.

❑   ❑ I save all my corrected homework to study from at test time.

Do you have some "Yes" answers? Great! Now see if you can turn some of your "No" answers into "Yes" answers. Start up some of the A+ good homework moves, one at a time.

Homework, Start to Finish

Homework begins at school, so what should be happening there homework-wise?

- **Ask the teacher to explain anything you don't understand *before* you leave class.** Sometimes students have problems with homework because they don't know quite what they are supposed to do once they get home. Most teachers are happy to repeat homework directions or work out examples again.

- **Recheck your assignment pad or planner and backpack before you leave school**. If you forget to bring your work or books home, see if you can get to school early the next day. Or use a free period to complete the missing assignment.

- **Get as much homework done at school as possible**. Use free time at school or during any after-school programs to finish up as much homework as you can so you have more free time at home.

You get home. The refrigerator is calling your name. So are your computer games. The phone is ringing. There's the remote. What's on television? Homework is pretty far down on the list of things you want to do as soon as you walk in the door. Then don't do it right away. Get out that timer. Give yourself some unwinding time and snack time. After you've been in the middle grades a bit, you'll soon have an idea of how much time you need to knock off all your homework. Here are some ways to manage the work that followed you home:

- **Set aside a block of time every day just for homework**. When you do your homework isn't as important as making time for it. Some days you can wrap it up in a free period. Other times you might want to see friends during your free period, so you'll do your homework at home. Schedule realistic time periods that work best for you.

- **Check your calendar every day for long-term assignments**. A long-term, two-week deadline shrinks fast. Look at your big calendar every day to see what's coming up soon. Get started on a few small steps for all your big projects.

- **Work on the hardest homework first . . . maybe**. Use your maximum brainpower for your hardest homework. Usually people have the most energy and concentration at the beginning of a task. However, there are some students who need to do easier work first just to get their wheels going. Try working both ways to see which method works better for you.

- **Use your timer to follow the A+ 20/10 Homework Method**. Set your timer for 20 minutes. Work for that amount of time without any interruptions. When your timer goes off, reset it for 10 minutes, and take a 10-minute break. Then start another 20-minute round of work with a 10-minute break until all your homework is finished. Find relaxing things you can do in 10 minutes. Tape a program for later. Check phone or e-mail messages to answer during your next 10-minute break. Get a glass of water and snack. Imitate a couch potato. Walk outside for 10 minutes. Do some stretches. Listen to music. Ten-minute breaks are fantastic ways give yourself a boost for the next 20-minute home-work session. You'll be amazed at how much work you can knock off using the A+ 20/10 Homework Method.

- **Work in different locations**. Memory experts have discovered something incredible about how students remember information. In studies on memory, college students seemed to remember more if they switched study locations for each subject. This is good news. Now you don't have to be a prisoner in your room while you do homework. So change the scenery if you can find a couple of quiet study spots around the house.

- **Review each assignment after you finish it**. Take this short extra step to check that there are no examples or words missing. See if you have all the right punctuation and spelling. Neatness counts for a lot. Recopy any sloppy work. Teachers usually don't give points for spaghetti spots.

- **Check your homework against the directions on the handout or your**

assignment planner. Did you do what your teacher assigned?

- **Put your homework and books in your backpack**. You know the drill. The backpack goes where you'll see it right away even if you oversleep the next morning.

- **Go have fun.** You're home free and homework-free.

- **If you get poor marks on homework, find out why**. Ouch! It's painful to get homework back with negative comments. See your teacher right away to get help.

- **Save all your homework**. You may never want to see those awful pages and pages of fractions again. But homework papers are some of the best study tools for future quizzes and exams. At test time, read over your old homework papers. See where you made mistakes. Here's an inside tip. *Believe it or not, teachers often take test questions right from the previous homework*. So store your homework in your notebook, or in those special subject folders at home.

Problem Homework

If homework was easy, you'd be hearing kids say: "Gee, no, I'd rather stay here and do my homework instead of going to a movie." Homework can be a drag. But sometimes it can be a real problem as well. What do you do when you're stuck on homework?

- **Mark sections with sticky notes next to homework that you don't understand**. A lot of students turn in poor homework because they get stuck on a problem. Or they don't understand the directions. Sometimes they're too afraid to tell the teacher about the problems they had. First, ask a parent or a study-buddy classmate to help you out. Or check a homework helper Web site. If you're still stuck, write a note to your teacher asking for help on the parts you couldn't do. Attach the note to your homework. Go to class a few minutes early. Show your teacher the homework you did do. Ask for help on the rest. See if you can get one more night to complete the assignment. Or if you have a free period later, see if you can bring in the assignment at the end of the day. These are all steps to try when you hit the homework wall. Just make sure you talk to your teacher *before* you turn in an incomplete assignment.

- **Complete all the homework that you can**. Reread your assignment pad, class notes, or the part of your textbook that applies to your homework. You might find the answers in one of those places.

- **Do what you can on the problem homework first**. Take a break. Then work on your easier homework. Later on, go back to what you didn't understand. A problem might be easier to solve the second time around.

Procrastination

What's worse than facing homework after school? Facing it hours later when it's time for bed! Pushing off jobs is called *procrastination*. Most people procrastinate once in a while. Some students push off work because they want their work to be so perfect, they're afraid to start. Others wait too long because they don't know how long a project will take. Some students don't understand the work and give up. Or they have so much work, they don't know where to begin. If you find yourself delaying work once in a while, you're normal! But if you regularly push schoolwork to the last minute because you can't face it, try some of these steps:

- **Reread Chapter 5 about what to do when a subject is too hard**.

- **Do a little on your easiest subject.** If you're in delay mode because you dread working on a hard subject, then don't. Try something easier just to get your brain in gear.

- **Ask a friendly someone to estimate how long a project or an assignment should take.** Knowing you can knock something off faster than you thought can help you pick up the pencil. If the assignment is a long one, ask that friendly someone to help you break down the work into smaller tasks.

- **Brainstorm.** Put your head together with someone else's when you need to find writing or project subjects. Just start talking about the assignment. Talking *is* getting work done! That someone can be a librarian, your teacher, an older student or sibling, a parent, or a friend. If you have science or history projects, watch a science or history show or DVD to get ideas. If you don't understand a book, go online to see if there's a summary of it. If you're stumped on math problems, go to a computer math Web site for middle graders and try to work out similar problems online.

- **Figure out how to start.** If you don't know how to begin, ask an adult what the first few steps are. Then do those steps until you get the hang of it.

- **Reward yourself.** "Okay, I'll memorize those facts for 10 minutes, then I'm going to play ball with my dog for 10 minutes."

- **Shorten the A+ 20/10 Method.** Yep, that again. If you're procrastinating, set your timer for 10 minutes, not 20 minutes, just to get going. Take a 5-minute mini-break, then work another 10/5

round. You can always increase your
time once you get started.

- **Do *something*.** That something can be
going to your favorite study spot and
just taking out one book and reading
the first paragraph. That something
can be doing one problem, one sentence, and one step. The brain works in
funny ways. It sometimes gets you "in
the groove" if you just push the Start
button.

How to Read Textbooks

To qualify as a textbook, a book has to weigh
at least two pounds and cause bulges in your
book bag! They make for heavy carrying and
heavy reading. Here is how to lighten the textbook reading load:

- **When you first get a textbook, read
the Table of Contents**. The Table of
Contents in front of the textbook gives
you the "big picture." It shows you—in
a shortcut way—what the *whole* book
is about. If you haven't done this yet
with the textbooks you have now, read

the Table of Contents before your next reading assignment. Why? Because this tells you what has been covered already and what's coming up. This will help you fit new information into a special slot.

- **Read all the heavy black titles in a reading assignment twice.** Do this once before you start the main reading and once after you have read the material. These headings are clues about what you will be reading or have just read.

- **Read any questions listed at the end of the chapter *before* you read.** This might sound like a backward way of doing things, but here's the reason. End-of-chapter questions alert you to important information and ideas in the reading.

- **Read the following twice**: Words in heavy black type such as titles and headings. First and last paragraphs of each section under the heavy black type. Charts and pictures. If the information in these images weren't important, the company that printed the book wouldn't hire an artist or photographer to illustrate it.

- **Read through most of your reading assignments just once**. If you review the Table of Contents, heavy type, opening and closing paragraphs, study all pictures and charts, and end-of-chapter questions, a onceover reading of everything else should do the job. Of course, if you don't understand the material, a second reading can help.

- **Write one or two sentences summing up the reading in your own words.** Keep these chapter summaries with your class notes. They'll be a big help at test time.

- **Look up words you don't understand in your dictionary**. Keep a student dictionary by your side whenever you read, or check an online student dictionary.

- **Write down page numbers and sections you don't understand**. If you are confused by some information, make a note of it to ask your teacher the next day.

How to Read Stories and Novels

These are usually the easiest and most enjoyable books to read. Read through fiction (made-up stories, plays, novels) once. If you don't understand what you have read, skim the material fast, then once more, slowly. Use your dictionary to look up words you don't know.

When you finish a reading assignment on this kind of book, ask yourself, or have someone ask these few questions: "Who were the main characters (the most important people in this part of the book)?" "What were the three most important things that happened?" "What is going to happen next?" If reading is a struggle for you, see if the library has an audio version of the book or movie you can listen to or watch.

7

How To Become a Great Test-Taker

There you are sailing along in school. You've gotten pretty organized at home and in class. Your locker could pass an Army inspection. Your notebook is as neat as a filing cabinet. Your homework assignments have been coming back with smiley faces on them.

Then, bam! Your teacher announces the first big test. Suddenly you can't remember one single thing you learned. Butterflies crash around in your stomach. Until that test is over, you are convinced you will not have a single moment of fun.

You don't even know where to begin. Are you supposed to read your whole textbook all over again? Memorize every word you ever wrote down in class? Here's what some experts—actual middle grade students— answered when they were asked: "What advice would you give new middle school students about taking tests?"

> *"Ask the teacher what is going to be on the test."*
> *"Study ahead of time."*
> *"Don't cram."*
> *"Study with a friend and quiz each other ahead of time."*
> *"Start studying early. Do a little bit at a time."*
> *"Don't throw out any papers the teacher gave you."*
> *"Do your work all the time. Don't let it pile up."*
> *"Memorize the important stuff."*
> *"Don't be nervous!"*

So how do you go about *not* being nervous? First, keep up all the good habits you may already have. Then think of some new ones that you could use. Here's a quiz to sort out what needs fixing from what doesn't.

Quiz Yourself on Test-Taking:

Check "Yes" or "No" next to each item below.

YES NO

❑   ❑   I always write down test dates in my assignment planner.

❑   ❑   Before I leave class I know what is going to be covered on the test.

❑   ❑   I copy the test date in huge letters on my calendar at home.

❑   ❑   I make up a plan to study for the test a few minutes every night, then longer the night before.

❑   ❑   I try not to make any plans the night before a test.

❑   ❑   My study plan includes:

❑   ❑   gathering and rereading all my old class notes, handout sheets, old tests, and homework papers.

❑   ❑   skimming my textbook and reading end-of-chapter questions.

❑   ❑   memorizing.

❑   ❑   quizzing myself the night before.

❑ ❑ I arrive in class with everything my teacher said to bring for the test.

❑ ❑ I listen carefully to the teacher's directions. I know how long I have, how many questions have to be answered, and whether to use pen or pencil.

❑ ❑ I write down my name and the date the very first thing.

❑ ❑ I read the main directions twice.

❑ ❑ I skim the whole test to see what I have to do.

❑ ❑ I figure out how much time I have to spend on each question.

❑ ❑ I read each question carefully before I answer it.

❑ ❑ I work on the easiest, most valuable problems first to give myself as many points as possible.

❑ ❑ I go back and answer any questions I skipped.

❑ ❑ I double-check my answers. I don't change them unless I have a good reason.

❑ ❑ I listen carefully when the teacher goes over my corrected test. Or I go over it myself to learn from my mistakes.

❑ ❑ I save all my old tests as study sheets for final exams.

❑ ❑ If I get a low grade, I meet with my teacher to find out why I lost points. I ask if I can retake the test or do an extra-credit project.

Do you do some of these test-prep and test follow-up steps? Great! Now add a few more good habits to your list. Here are the important steps all test-takers should follow along with information about why the steps help.

Pretest Shape-up

- **Write down the test date**. This is your first step in getting ready for a test. Once you know the date, figure out how many days you have to study for it.

- **Find out what is going to be covered on the test**. If a math test is going to include only long division, spend all your practice time on that, not on fractions or multiplication.

- **Listen for clues in class**. Teachers *want* you to do as well on tests as you can. Often in the days before a big test, a teacher will go over what the class has been studying. This is the time to get your notes up to date or to underline important parts of the notes you already have. If your science teacher keeps repeating the word *camouflage*, that probably means you are going to be tested on it.

At-Home Shape-Up

- **Copy your test date on a big calendar.**

- **Play catch-up a few nights ahead.** Set aside a few minutes a night to catch up on missing work. Go over old homework, handouts, and quizzes. If there are parts of the work you don't understand, get help while there's still time. Start memorizing what your teacher said to memorize.

- **Skim your textbook.** Look at the Table of Contents for the chapter that is going to be on the test, the boldface headings, opening and closing paragraphs, and especially the end-of-chapter questions. Often teachers ask questions that are like those.

- **Reread anything that looks important in the book or in your notebook.**

- **Think up your own questions.** See if you can answer them in your head. This is a great step to do with a study buddy.

- **Ask someone to quiz you the night before.** Or quiz yourself to see if you know the information inside out.

- **Line up everything you will need for the test**.

- **Go to bed early so you will be rested the next day.** Have a good breakfast the day of the test.

Memorizing Tips

- **Know what facts you are supposed to memorize.**

- **Make up flash cards for important facts.** Write the fact in big letters on one side of the card and the explanation of the fact on the other side. Quiz yourself on your flash cards, or have someone else quiz you.

- **Or picture what you have to memorize.** Make mind maps of facts that go together.

- **Reread, or say out loud, what you are trying to memorize.** Hearing information aloud, even out of your own mouth, is a great way to get the information to stick. If you get tired of talking to yourself, record the information into an audio device and play it back. Use playbacks to memorize spelling and vocabulary lists or math, science, or social studies facts.

- **Memorize a little each day**. Repetition really helps.

- **Work on memorization early in your homework period.** That's when your mind is most alert.

- **Get plenty of zzzs.** One of the most important jobs of sleep is to lay down information in memory areas of the brain. You can ask sleep-lab rats that! Several sleep studies show that rats dream about mazes they traveled during the day.

Test-Time Tips

If you have done most of these steps, you're good to go. What's next?

- **Arrive early and have what you need**. Give yourself a little extra time on test day so you don't feel rushed. Bring extra pens, pencils, scrap paper, and an eraser to class. If you feel nervous in spite of everything, try these relaxers. Take deep breaths and let them out slowly. Or doodle on a scrap of paper. Or slowly clench and unclench muscles head to toe.

- **Listen carefully to your teacher.** Make sure you know how long you have for the test and what you're supposed to do. Should you use pen or pencil? Is scrap paper allowed for figuring or notes? Can you use a dictionary or calculator? If you are not sure about the spoken directions, ask your teacher to repeat them.

- **Write your name and date on the paper first thing.**

- **Skim the whole test.** This will give you an idea of what the whole test is about.

- **Read any written directions slowly.** Underline parts of the directions that seem important. Before you write anything, you should know how much time you have; how many questions you are supposed to answer; what each section is worth so that you can spend the most time on the most valuable questions.

- **Try to answer a question in your head before reading the choices.** You may already know the answers to many multiple choice, fill-in, or true or false questions. When you read a test question, and a definite answer pops into your head, look for the choice that best matches your answer.

- **Wrong answers often include certain words.** In multiple choice or true or false questions, absolute words such as *never*, *always*, *least*, *most*, and *none* are often in the *wrong* answer.

- **Answer the easiest of the most valuable questions first.** Once you knock those off, go back to the beginning and tackle the next-easiest of the most-valuable questions.

- **Reread harder questions.** Underline important words to help yourself understand the question better. Don't get stuck on a question. Move on to questions you can answer until you have gotten through all of those. Your goal is to gain as many points as possible.

- **Guess answers.** If you are going to get the same number of points taken off for an incomplete answer, then you might as well take a good guess at it. Maybe you'll get some credit for part of your answer.

- **Make a mind map or mini-outline on scrap paper for essay questions.** On a piece of scrap paper or in the margin, clump together facts in a mind map or list to back up opinions you want to write about. Then write a strong sentence stating your opinion. Support it with the facts from your mind map or list.

- **Check that you have done every example**. It's frustrating to lose points because you skipped a question by mistake.

- **Reread your answers to make sure they are correct and complete.** Don't change any answers unless you have at least one good reason for doing so.

After the Test

Learn from your successes and mistakes. Go over your corrected test carefully. Notice what you did well. What mistakes did you make? Figure out why you made them. Did you have problems with the material? Or just misunderstand some part of the question? Next time around, spend extra study time on the problems that tripped you up. Either study more or take extra care on the test itself. Save your corrected tests. Use them as study tools for finals.

Go have fun. You deserve it!

8
What's on Your Mind?
Answers to Student Questions

What are kids really worried about when it comes to surviving the middle grades? What problems would they like to fix? Here are some problems middle graders like you asked about.

Making Decisions

QUESTION: *I can't make decisions—even about small things! Some days I can't even decide what to wear or what to have for lunch. Lots of times I can't make up my mind about which homework to do first. Then, by the time I decide, it's too late. Help!*

ANSWER: Guess what? Decisions don't have to be perfect, just acceptable. Making acceptable decisions takes practice. Whenever you have to decide something, make sure you have all the information you need. Give yourself a few minutes to think of the plusses and minuses. Then go with the plus side. Here are some tips on making decisions about common school problems:

- **Deciding what to wear.** Find out the weather forecast each night. Think about whether you have gym or some other special activity the next day. Based on the weather and your plans for the next day, choose the outfit that you like best. Stick with your decision in the morning. It's probably just fine!

- **Deciding what to have for lunch.** Do you bring your own lunch and you can't decide what to make? List your four favorite lunches. Have your parents stock one favorite per week for four weeks, then start the cycle again. Do you buy lunch at school? Schools usually publish menus a week ahead. Go over the menus at home where things are less chaotic. Pick out the favorite meal for each day of the week and stick with it.

- **Deciding which homework to do first.** Do the most difficult homework first to get it out of the way. Some students, though, like to warm up with easier homework. Figure out your homework style and stick with it if it's working.

Too Many Subjects, Too Many Teachers

QUESTION: *Sometimes I wish I could go back to a lower grade. I had only one main teacher then, and she didn't give us as much homework. I have so many teachers now, it took me a week to learn their names. Sometimes they all pile on the homework the same night or give tests on the same day. How can I keep all these classes straight?*

ANSWER: It's hard to see new faces and deal with new personalities every 40 minutes or so. And it's even harder to keep track of so much different work. Teachers aren't always aware of conflicts. If you feel comfortable with your teacher, let her know that the math teacher has a big test planned the same day as your science test. If that's too hard to do, then check your calendar for upcoming tests and projects. Try to figure out separate study schedules for each test or project. Set aside the most time for the hardest subject. Another possibility is to study with one or two other people in class. Break down the big study job into smaller steps. One of you can get the class notes up to date. Another person can make up possible test questions and flash cards. One person can do the heavy-duty reading and take notes for the rest of you. Sharing jobs like this will give you each more time to study for any conflicting tests.

Bad Report Card

QUESTION: *The last time I came home with a bad report card, my parents went crazy. I'm trying to do better at school, but I'm scared of what will happen if I get bad grades again. I feel like running away from home.*

ANSWER: Don't run away! First, read this book and follow some of the suggestions in it to improve your grades. It may take a little time before your grades improve. Meanwhile, here's what to do about a bad report card you know is coming. If there are still a few weeks left, ask your teachers if you can do extra work you to pull up your grades. Sometimes teachers allow students to retake a test, write an extra paper, or make up missing homework. Then talk to your parents right away. Tell them you think you might be getting a bad grade and that you have already started doing something about it. They won't be as likely to get upset if you tell them your study plans.

Interfering Parents

QUESTION: *I turn in some of the best homework and reports in my class. Know why? My parents do a lot of it for me! It's not as much fun as you might think either. If I get a good grade, I don't feel that great about it because it's not really mine. Sometimes I get a bad grade on work I do in class because I'm so used to having my parents do it better. How can I get them to stop butting in?*

ANSWER: This is a common problem and hard to cure. Parents are sometimes too eager to share what they know. Sometimes the interference starts when parents supervise homework, then fix errors themselves. This makes it hard for students to learn from mistakes. Sometimes parents change the work so much it doesn't really belong to their child anymore. The homework is yours. The grades are yours. Tell your parents it's okay for them to check your work but that you want to be responsible for doing it. Let them know that you will learn the material better if you do the actual work yourself. If this is still a problem, do a lot of your homework at school and leave it there.

Lateness

QUESTION: *No matter what I do, I'm always late for everything. Now that I have so many classes, the problem is even worse.*

ANSWER: Here are some things to help you get to where you're going on time:

- **Figure out how long things take.** Maybe you think washing your hair takes 3 minutes, but you take 10 minutes. Time all your at-home routines as you do them to get a realistic idea of how long they take so you can budget your time.

- **Your timer is your friend.** Give yourself mini-deadlines to complete certain jobs. For example, give yourself 10 minutes to shower; 10 minutes to get dressed; 20 minutes for breakfast, and so on. You may find yourself running on time or even a little ahead. After a while, you won't need the timer.

- **Set your own deadlines.** Take charge of your own schedule rather than depending on other people to make you be on time.

- **Follow the same routine every day.** Get up at the same time. Put your clothes and books in the same place. Finish breakfast by a certain time, and so on.

Asking for Help

QUESTION: *All my teachers ever seem to do is pile on the work or lecture me about stuff I forgot to do. Sometimes they can be nice, but a lot of the time I'm afraid of my teachers. If only they could read my mind.*

ANSWER: Even the best teachers can't read the minds of all their students. So it's up to you to talk to them, one to one, and share what's on your mind. This isn't always easy since teachers and students in middle school have such busy schedules. What a lot of students don't realize is that there are ways of talking over problems with teachers before they get to a crisis. Here are a few ways to get a teacher on your side:

- **If you miss an assignment, or you know you did a poor job, go to class a little early and tell the teacher right away.** Most teachers find out these things only when they are correcting papers at home and you're not there to explain yourself. Tell your teacher— honestly—why you are missing some homework or couldn't do a good job on it. Ask for help. Offer a plan for redoing or making up the work. Most teachers will be very impressed by a student who goes halfway like this.

- **Don't wait until the report card comes out to see your teacher if you're struggling.** Every time you get a low grade on a test or paper, see your teacher right away to find out how you can improve next time. Teachers are there to help you, but they can't help if they don't know there's a problem.

- **Be a bit of a goody goody.** Even if an assignment is really hard, do some of it to show you're trying. Some behaviors are "freebies." They don't require any special knowledge or brain cells. Be on time. Behave in class. Have your materials with you all the time. Answer questions in class once in a while. These habits don't cost a thing but pay off big time. If you score points on attitude, your teacher is much more likely to be on your side at report card time.

Kids Who Tease

QUESTION: *Sometimes I hate going to school. I like my teachers and my friends, but lots of*

times certain kids bug me in the hallways or in
the playground. How can I get them to stop?

ANSWER: You have a right to stand up for yourself if someone bugs you, touches you, or takes your stuff. Step forward, push your shoulders back, look the annoying person in the eye, then say: "Cut it out. That's teasing, it's mean, so knock it off." Then walk the other way just as if you saw a snaggle-toothed dog across the street.

You can sometimes surprise a teaser or bully with a quick comeback. Bully: "You're an idiot." You: "Oh, thanks for letting me know. I'll work on it." Then step away. Do that two or three more times if the person keeps bugging or bullying you. If it keeps happening, report the person to your favorite teacher. No one has the right to insult you, shove you around, or take your property. And don't forget the instant invisibility cloak. When you spot the teasers on the horizon, imagine they are wearing something that makes them invisible. You just don't see them!

Problem Friends

QUESTION: *I do okay in school, but my best friends goof off. I want them to stay friends with me, but they tease me about being teacher's pet just because I get good grades. What can 1 do?*

ANSWER: Try to enjoy these friends as much as you can out of school and during free periods. Maybe some of them are having problems in school. Invite them over to study together. If your friends still tease you about school, get friendly with a couple of other kids who are more like you. After a while you won't have to depend on your old friends as much. Good luck!

Cramming

QUESTION: *Why do I always start cramming the night before?*

ANSWER: Crammers like to tell themselves that if only they'd had the time, they would have gotten 100 instead of 72 on a test. Or an A + instead of a C. Students who cram are often the same ones who put things off. Cramming is the surest way to wreck your appetite, your sleep, and your peace of mind. So avoid cramming. Instead, do a little bit of the work each day no matter what it is.

Now that that's settled, here's some advice on how to cram. Use only in case a meteorite lands on your backpack, or you fall asleep for two years and wake up the night before a big exam. Here goes:

- **Find a place to study with zero distractions.** Give yourself at least one hour to study.

- **Skim all your class notes and handout sheets.**

- **Skim over the sections of your textbook that you were supposed to study for the test.**

- **Write down a word or two about important ideas as you read.**

- **Read facts and definitions out loud a few times each.**

- **If you are taking a math test, quickly work out two or three examples from the book.**

- **Go to bed at your normal time and get up at your normal time.** Losing sleep is only going to make that jumble of information worse.

- **Get to class early.** Do some slow, deep breathing to calm your nerves.

- **After you take the test, promise yourself you will never cram again—ever!**

Cheating

QUESTION: *One of my friends gets good grades by cheating on tests. Her parents are really strict about school, so she's afraid of getting bad grades. Once or twice she asked me to cheat, too, when we sat next to each other. I pretended not to hear her. It sure makes me mad when she gets a better grade than I do. Tell me what to do.*

ANSWER: Keep saying no to the cheating. Sooner or later, your friend is going to get caught, and you won't want to be any part of that. She may want you to join her to make her cheating seem okay. It's not okay. Maybe your friend doesn't really know how to prepare for a test on her own. You might suggest studying together as an alternative.

Studying with a Friend

QUESTION: *My best friend and I try to study for tests together, but we always wind up talking, laughing, or eating instead. I think we sometimes do worse on tests than if we studied alone. I thought studying with another person was supposed to help you out on tests. Should we keep studying together?*

ANSWER: Try studying together only if you can *really* do the following:

- **Catch up on all your work separately.** A day or two before you meet, both you and your friend should review all your old notes and the material that will be covered on the test.

- **Do all your memorization before the two of you get together.**

- **Separately write down a couple of questions you think the teacher might ask.**

- **Promise each other to spend at least half an hour studying for the test**. Set aside this half hour at the beginning of the visit.

- **Spend fifteen minutes reading over each other's class notes, old home-work, and tests.**

- **Spend the last fifteen minutes quiz-zing each other.** Ask each other the questions you each made up.

- **After the half hour is over, relax and hang out.** Go to the kitchen. Get a snack. Spend at least a half hour hanging!

Nervous About Tests

QUESTION: *Even though I study for tests, I'm a nervous wreck when I have to take one. My heart starts pounding. I drop my pencil. I for-get what I studied. My mind goes blank. How can I calm down?*

ANSWER: A little nervousness is a good thing. It gets your mind in gear and gives you a spurt of energy. It does sound as if your nervousness is causing problems, though. First, think about what's making you nervous. Are you worried about getting a bad grade? Are you afraid if you don't do well your parents will get mad? Do you think you have to get a great grade every time? Keep this in mind: test scores are only one part of your final grade. Repeat to yourself: "Homework, answering questions in class, and my behavior in class count as much as this test."

Now that you know that tests are just one part of your grade, here are some other tips to calm yourself:

- **Follow the study tips in Chapter 7 of this book.** Those test-taking tips will give you a great foundation for the test.

- **Study a little bit at a time.** Avoid cramming the night before or the morning of the test. Rushing and cramming set off worries and nervousness.

- **Go to sleep and get up at the regular time on test day.** Being rested calms you down.

- **Get to class a little early.** But don't cram during those extra minutes. Instead, close your eyes or daydream about something soothing—waves lapping on a shore or someone rubbing your forehead. Or slowly doodle on a piece of paper. Or clench your fists, then very slowly unclench them. Do all this before the teacher starts talking or hands out the test. If you find yourself getting tense during the test, try one of these exercises again to relax yourself.

- **Have a plan for doing the test.** Do the easiest examples first to build your self-confidence. (If some sections are worth more than others, do the easiest of the most valuable questions first.)

- **Don't get stuck on a question.** That will just make you more nervous. Move right on to something you can answer. You can always go back later.

Remember, it's only a test. The rest of your class work and participation count for a lot, too.

9

Quick Review: A School Survival Kit

What do you do when you need to get in shape for school fast? When you want to change those C's to B's or A's? When you are determined to catch up on your homework once and for all? Or when you just want to get off to a good start as the new semester begins? This School Survival Kit lists a few shortcuts to get yourself on track quickly. Check it out whenever you need help in a hurry.

School Tools

- Three-ring notebook with subject dividers or different colored notebooks for each class

- Assignment pad
- Extra class schedules (home, notebook, locker)
- Extra supplies—three-ring notebook paper, extra pens and pencils—half at home, half in your locker
- Phone number of a student in each class
- Library card
- Dictionary
- Book bag or backpack
- Bulletin board or white board at home
- Large wall calendar for appointments and deadlines
- Timer
- Wristwatch and alarm clock
- Tape recorder
- Thesaurus and dictionary
- Earplugs

Listening Skills Checklist

- Do all your work before going to class.
- Be on time.

- Open your notebook when you sit down.
- Make eye contact with the teacher.
- Listen for clues to main ideas.
- Listen for repetition, rephrasing, and summaries.
- Stay involved by asking or answering questions.
- Take notes.

Note-Taking Skills Checklist

- Write the date on each set of notes and handout sheets.
- Draw a line or fold your notebook sheet 3 inches from left edge.
- Write main ideas or questions on the left.
- List related ideas on the right.
- Underline important words in your notes and on handouts.
- Save handout sheets in the proper section of your notebook or file them at home.

- When the teacher says, "Write it down," write it down.

- Copy what the teacher puts on the blackboard.

- If you miss a class, borrow someone else's notes and get the handout sheets.

- Read each day's notes when you do your homework.

- Reread all notes and handouts covered on a test.

Homework Skills Checklist

In Class:

- Write down each assignment and due date.
- Ask questions when you don't understand the homework.

- Know what books and materials you need to take home that day.

At Home:

- Write down long-term deadlines and test days on a big wall calendar.

- Check your wall calendar every day.
- Figure out the best time of day to do homework.
- Work on the hardest homework first unless you need to warm up with easy homework.
- If you get stuck, try this:

Reread your class notes, handouts, or book to see if the answer is in one of those places.

Move on to other homework. Then go back to the hard part.

Call a classmate or ask a family member for help.

Test-Taking Checklist

- Find out what material will be covered on the test.
- Copy the test date onto a big calendar.
- Plan a study schedule so that you do a little each day. Set aside a longer amount of time on the two nights before the test.

- Catch up on missing assignments and notes right away.
- Do your memorizing a little bit at a time every day.
- Skim your class notes and handout sheets.
- Skim old tests and homework assign ments.
- Skim your textbook chapters.
- Answer questions at the end of chapters in your head.
- Ask for help on any material you don't understand.
- Think of a few questions the teacher might ask and answer them in your head.
- Quiz yourself the night before, or study with a friend and quiz each other.
- Go to bed on time. Have a good breakfast on test day. Bring what you will need to school.
- Arrive a little early with all your materials—extra paper, pens, pencils, and an eraser.

- Listen carefully to the teacher's directions.

- Write your name and the date on the test sheet.

- Read carefully any written directions, underlining important words as you read.

- Figure out a quick schedule of how much time to spend on each question.

- Devote more time to questions that are worth the most.

- Leave a few minutes at the end for rereading the test.

- See if you can answer the questions before you look at the choices. Then match them up.

- Work on the easiest, most valuable questions first.

- Go back to the harder questions.

- Guess answers if you have to.

- When you have finished, check that you did each question.

- Reread the test to make sure you haven't made any mistakes.

- Check that your paper is neat and easy to read.

- Don't change any answers unless you have at least one good reason for doing so.

- Save all your tests to learn from your mistakes and your strengths.

Top Tips from Students Who Made It Through the Middle Grades and Lived to Tell About It

"Don't wait until the last minute.
"Start studying early."
"Write everything, but everything,
down. It's the only way you'll
remember what you're supposed to."
"Reread everything you do."
"Don't throw out anything your
teacher hands out."
"Don't worry. Just do it."
"Take notes and keep them where
you can find them. Handouts, too."
"Be on time no matter what."
"Don't worry if you don't make
friends the first day."
"It gets easier, so hang in there."

About the Author

Louise Colligan, soon to be known as Mizz C. on the Internet, became the author of many study skill books after she saw how confusing the middle grades could be for her students. What followed was a series called the *A+ Guides*, which she recently updated.

And get this. Mizz C. has gone digital. Yes, the *A+ Guide to Great Grades* is available in print and on the Internet. (Mizz C. wonders how a book can really be a book if you can't turn the pages, but her young geek friends say this is now possible. They also say her book will be readable on a cell phone, but she doesn't believe it.)

Stayed tuned for future updated books in the *A+ Series*. Next up? *The A+ Guide to Great Test Taking* and the *A+ Guide to Great Writing*. Check out Mizz C's brand new blog at aplusguides. blogspot.com/ and her Facebook page. Coming soon is Mizz C's aplusguides.com website. Watch out, she may even start Tweeting or Twittering if someone shows her how. Keep on Googling until Mizz C. makes her debut! "Coming soon," her tech wizards say.

Index

www.ingramcontent.com/pod-product-compliance
Lightning Source LLC
Chambersburg PA
CBHW050536280326
41933CB00011B/1606